Rose Petals Floating Downstream

Spiritual poetry to uplift the soul

ANITA NEILSON

First published 2018.

Text copyright: Anita Neilson 2018.

ISBN: 978-1-72917-407-8

(Paperback)

Imprint: Independently published

Endorsements:

"This tender poetry collection, *Rose Petals Floating Downstream,* guides us on a journey of self-reflection and transformation. Anita Neilson's beautiful words express the many experiences of life, reminding us to slow down and re-connect to the ever-changing beauty within and around us. This book is wonderful spiritual companion and support through life."

Karen Lang, Author, *Courage.*
https://www.karenlangauthor.com/

"I found tremendous comfort in the author's gentle prose. *Rose Petals Floating Downstream* is a collection of poems to savor over and over."

Jill Weatherholt, Author, *Harlequin Love Inspired.* https://jillweatherholt.wordpress.com/

"*Rose Petals Floating Downstream* lures the reader with gracious comfort than catches you up with a startling phrase like "Soft silken raindrops/ alight on my soul/ as

i

the dance of life begins/ and you curl around
my core." (On Angels' Wings). Anita
Neilson's spiritual poetry is solace for a
fractious world. Jump in."

Rita Kowats, Spiritual Guide, Author of
blog, *Spirituality Without Borders*.
http://spiritualitywithoutborders.blog/

Other books by the Author:

Acts of Kindness from your Armchair,
Ayni Books 2017. ISBN: 978-1-
78535-617-9

An exploration of how we can make a
meaningful contribution to the world through
simple acts of kindness, all easily done from
home. The book acts as a practical guide to the
ways in which thoughts, words and acts of
kindness, both inward and towards the wider
world, can create real change. This toolkit of
ideas and practices arose from the author's
personal experiences in her quest to find a new
purpose in life, despite health limitations,
through the power of kindness.

"We can all make a difference, regardless of
any 'limitations' we may have, whatever our
circumstances. In my experience all 'big'
things happen through lots of small things, and
this book is a great reminder of the big
difference that small everyday acts of kindness
can make." Karen Darke MBE, Athlete and

Adventurer, Paralympic Champion 2016.
Author of *If You Fall* and *Boundless*.

"A spiritual guidebook for harmonious living." Catherine L. Schweig, Editor of *Bhakti Blossoms, Journey of the Heart* and others.

"Inspires the reader to achieve a happier, more fulfilled living and open up to positivity, peace and natural wellbeing." Fotoula Adrimi, Director ISIS School of Holistic Health.

"This is great for people who want to help but have no idea where to start." Dawn's Reviews.

Goddess When She Rules, Golden Dragonfly Press 2017. ISBN: 9780998976655

Contributing Author in this extraordinary collection of poetry and prose penned by spiritual women across the globe in an exploration of what the Goddess energy signifies to them.

COMING SOON (July 2019)

Soul Murmurs: Seasonal words of spiritual wisdom to enlighten the soul, O-Books. ISBN: 978-1-78904-111-8

A must-have collection of poetry and prose imbued with spiritual wisdom from east and west. Gathered under seasonal headings to echo the eternal cycle of life, each page resonates with peace and calm, offering comfort and moments of reflection in a fast-moving world.

Acknowledgements:

Biblical quotations are from The King James Authorised Version of 1611.

Quotations from *The Interior Castle* by St Teresa of Avila, are from the 1911 edition by The Benedictines of Stanbrook, revised and edited by very Rev. Benedict Zimmerman.

The image *Bluebell Haze* is used with the kind permission of the artist. jennybrownartist.com.

The image *Ocean-811410* by Natureworks, Pixabay.com, is used under the terms of the Creative Commons CCO public domain dedication licence.

Contents

Preface:

"To write is to feel the world
in its essence
every fibre of meaning extracted
to dance across the page,
enveloping the reader
in a languid embrace."
-Anita Neilson.

Around 9 years ago, I had a physical and emotional breakdown after decades of living in the fast lane. This hectic lifestyle in pursuit of perfection and must-have experiences finally caught up with me, and from that day hence my life changed dramatically, with ill-health being the primary focus. My body was wracked with a plethora of painful conditions. I was a mess, and felt very sorry for myself. After two years of living in a kind of *stasis*, a friend suggested I try a meditation class. I went along to make up the numbers…..and I loved it! Here was the peace I had been seeking for years. Here was a place I could really be myself, no more trying to be someone I thought everyone else wanted me to be. Here I could rediscover me.

Out of the midst of the nightmare of ill-health, the most beautiful, beatific font of poetry began to *flow through me*; I was not the author, but a co-writer if you like, editing lines, putting my spin on things. It was, and is, the most precious gift. When the words come, there is an urgency to them and I rush to write them down lest they disappear from the ether.   They flow when I am relaxed, in that state of inner peace which comes with meditation or in the drowsy state between sleep and wakefulness. It is at these times of inner stillness that I believe we come closest to the vast font of knowledge ever present in the ether (Akashic records) and are able to access it for creative purposes.

Writing poetry has been a way of recording my spiritual development from its tentative beginnings of surprised awakening, through the many stages of doubt, rationalisation and wonder. From finding myself immersed in a growing faith, peace and joy, firstly in the external world, and then as my meditation practice deepened, in the interior world, as I journeyed towards my soul self. St Teresa of Avila, a 16th century Carmelite nun and saint, was herself beset will illness, and yet she saw this challenge of ill-health as a potent example of God's grace: "Sometimes He calls souls by means of sickness or troubles".

The structure of this compilation reflects my spiritual journey. You will see that it is divided into four sections: The Natural World, The Play of Life, Transformation, and Prayer / Supplication. As you read, I hope you too will be transported from the exoteric to the esoteric: from the external, spiritual experiences in the natural world to the inner world of bliss and joy!

The poems cover such topics as:

- experiencing the Divine in the natural world;
- exploring the tenet of life on earth as being God's play, and we merely actors playing our part. These poems offer hope and advice on not being overly affected by life's challenges.

- The theme of transformation is covered in the third section, reflecting my own spiritual experiences as my meditation practice deepened and became more centred around contacting Source / God / the Divine / Krishna / Oneness;

- Deep longing for God is expressed in the prayer / supplication final section, as well as poetic verse of hope, resurrection and burning away of karma.

Why not take time out from the hectic pace of life in which we currently find ourselves. Hold a poem in your hands like a sacred gift and read it a few times to absorb its meaning for you. It may bring that spark of hope you were looking for, or transport you to a tranquil, distant land; it may offer advice or support through life's challenges; it may open your eyes and your heart to envelop all life around you with love. These beautiful poems may also be used as reading aids for spiritual development and meditation. Use them as you will, but most of all enjoy them!

The Natural World:

Rose Petals Floating Downstream

Lying here
blissful and serene
tranquil as a rose petal
floating downstream.

Gently swayed,
its essence conveyed
to the waters:
as in a dream.

Its wistful beauty reflected
in a cloudless sky;
Its languid joy
a contented sigh.

Stretching its form
each cell drenched in light.
Twirling and pausing,

bobbing and floating.
Each moment:
sheer delight.

Cast adrift, free,
it can simply be
a rose petal
floating downstream.

Day's frantic gasps for release

Galloping 'cross the night sky
pulled by invisible horsemen
on a journey
into daylight's embrace.
The moon's ethereal messengers
in this cosmic
dance of grace.

Sinuous threads
leave trails so bright
that she may swiftly follow,
casting ghost-like shadows
in the hollows of my mind.

Leaning back in my chair,
home to sleepless nights
too numerous to share,
a shuddering yawn
disrupts my reverie;

jolts me from sweet dreams

of make-believe

as the moonlit chariot

is swept from the scene

by day's frantic gasps for release.

Solstice Light

Lush green grass
spun by nature's wheel
trembles in dawn's eager light.
Solstice embers
of days remembered
fizzle out under dew's
watchful gaze.
The Sun God Ra flexes his limbs
coursing rays of love
all over this land,
and like flowers releasing
their night-borne scent
the shadows of my heart
unveil themselves
dispersing into ether
and transmuted into light.

Thou Art Mine!

"Everybody needs beauty as well as bread,

places to play in and pray in,

where nature may heal and give strength

to body and soul." - John Muir

O mountainous glory thou art mine!

whose velvet carpeting affords

soft repose to weary limbs;

whose lithesome wind

caresses each pore,

gladly surrendering;

where an outstretched hand

may touch infinity

and embrace it within.

Rose Petals Floating Downstream

O mountainous wonder thou art mine!

whose poets and artists

have long pondered life

and sought to imbue it with light;

whose skylines are traced

with creative imaginings

preserving God's masterpiece in time.

Earth Spirit

She moves in tune
with the wind
unseen by human eyes.
Her delicate veil
an endless trail
of fairy-soft steps
encircling the Earth.

Her breath is an Angel's kiss
light as the morning mist
caressing the skyline.
Her dance a melodic harmony
of light and form.
Earth Spirit rejoices
in this glorious morn.

She is maiden and mother
sister and friend
belonging to no-one and all.
Taste her in the air

after rainfall.
See her in the forest
flitting to and fro.
Hear her song
in the waterfall at dusk
when creatures
large and small
congress to hear her call.

Earth Spirit breathes calm
over all.
Earth Spirit breathes calm
on us all.
She breathes for us all.

The Bluebell Wood

(after a painting by Jenny Brown)

Sage-clad sentinels of the forest
keep watch o'er the bluebell wood
as a timeless dawn mist
eases her grip
on her treasure within.

Flexing their limbs
with each creak of the wind
streaking through gossamer veils,
these gentle giants

close ranks once again,
like grandparents
protecting their kin.

The sky's azure reflection
carpets all around,
dotted with scent-pods
of wild garlic flowers.
This feast for the senses
is paradise found:
Milton's antithesis
of sight and sound!

In this carefree playground
of nymphs and sprites
the bluebell bonnets
quiver with delight.
Life is in the giving!
O, to be alive is so good
this beautiful morning
in the bluebell wood!

The great hoose

(a poem in the Scots' tongue)

The great hoose
at the tap o' the brae
whaur prayers are spoke
for a' guid fowk.
Myne ye don't sin
or they'll no' let ye in!

The minister's cloak
like a toreador's cape
in the win' does blaw
welcoming you in—
but myne the sting behin'!

Some say witches fly
in the kirkyard at nicht
as gied such a fricht
tae pure Tam in Alloway Kirk.

The dew drops and the rose

The softest of landings
awaits the tiny dewdrops
scattered like diamonds
at daybreak's command.

Sweet scentsations
perfume the air
drenching all life
in their heady trails.

Rosa rugosa:
labyrinthine pleasure;
sweet journey within,
infusing all between
in a sandman's dream.

Tenderly held are
these tiny dewdrops
frozen in space

till sunlight's embrace

transports them

ether-bound;

and dawn once again

comes around.

Champagne Rain

Champagne rain
falls, needle-sharp,
on the embers
of my heart
torn asunder by desires.
Fill my cup with Thee.

Bubbles of pain
like howls of a wolverine
surface to complain
to the moon's icy gaze.
Fill my mind with Thee.

Throw me a life-belt
from these tundra-hewn thoughts.
Break through the ice
of this frozen north
where spiteful words
freeze on the tongue

and ears, muffled by pride,
hear not Your word.
Fill my heart with Thee.

Immerse me in the sweet
bubbles of Your love
that I may swim to Thee
drunk on the ecstasy
of blissful reunion.
Fill my soul with Thee!

Sun Rising

Sun rising
from the sleepy horizon
of its dormancy.
Golden atom split
by the arrow of time.
A new day is dawning.
Sunrays blinding
this temporal shift
from then to now.
Senses drowned
by the tidal wave of sounds.
A new day is dawning.
Body and soul bathing
in each wave of light
washing over and through.
Placid waters skimmed
leaving little trace
in the fabric of time.
A new day is dawning.

Fall's Gold

Autumnal light
folds inwards
resting easy on the skin.
Summer bounty
now Fall's gold
lies crushed underfoot:
dappled nuggets of plenty
peppering a resting world.

Copper tresses:
mellow rivers of sky fall
chase the sun earthbound
melting Winter's icy breath.

Denuded branches
play their song
to the breeze
lullabies of longing
to a resting world.

The Thaw

The thaw
when it comes
anticipatory glee
undone;
tumbling life-blossoms
revitalizing
showers of light.

Frozen rivers
groaning
contractions of re-birth
releasing icy cries
to the wailing wind.

Life ever-present
thrives 'neath
the surface,
as Spring's sighs
caress the mind

with "Get well soon" wishes

to a weary mankind.

The thaw

when it comes

celebratory toast,

popping bubbles

of joy

for the season of hope.

The Play of Life:

Grace brims over

"There are only two ways to live your life:

One is as though nothing is a miracle;

The other is as though everything

is a miracle." – Albert Einstein

Gratitude spills from these eyes

suffused with light

from the world outside,

but seeking wisdom within.

Grace brims over on these lips

sharing memories of old:

whispered longings

of the soul.

Love abounds for these feet

treading circles of life

bathed in peace:

each step closer to Thee.

Thanks overflows in this heart
beating perfect time
with the oneness of mankind,
fluttering on Angels' wings
to be by Your side.

Lord, I am re-born
-a curious observer
of this wondrous life -
on a spiralling adventure
like a fairground ride!

On Angels' Wings

Soft silken raindrops
alight on my soul
as the dance of life begins
and you curl around my core.
In the world, yet scarcely,
carried here on Angels' wings;
tenderly entwined are we
through life's ecstatic symphony.

Sweetest of teardrops
fall on your gaze
as my heart implodes with love
at your tiny embrace.
In the world, so bravely,
brought here by God's grace.

My restless heart no longer aches
as in drowsy contentment
I vow to love and protect you
each step of the way.

Ambassadors of Peace

Embracing life's path,
pearls of grace
trailing in their wake,
Ambassadors of Peace
walk in the world
but not for its sake.

Life's toils are swept aside
by the folds of their capes,
cloaked in wisdom
by love's translucent rays.
Ambassadors of Peace
work in the world
but not for its sake.

Torchlights of serenity,
unhurried by time,
scattering droplets
of kindness

to nurture mankind.
Ambassadors of Peace
serve in the world
for its sake.

Slow gentle waves
in a lake of tranquillity,
they teach peace and calm,
compassion and humility.
They light the way ahead,
they steer a steady course,
Ambassadors of Peace:
form a bridge back to Source.

You are Divine

You are Divine
a sublime reflection
of my love for you.
With you by my side
there is no time
no sense of yours or mine:
just us.

Ours is a joyous union
of body and soul
of hopes that take flight
in an endless night
of starlit dreams;
where love is the salve
for all life's ills;
and tender repairer
of hearts and minds.

You are heaven-sent
and earthly bound
yet our love is eternal.
Let's fly together
soaring in the updrafts,
trailing pearls of joy
in our wake.
Let's love together
sowing seeds of contentment
to root where they may.
Let's be together
in sublime, blissful union.

I give you my heart,
my soul, my mind.
You are my friend, my love.
You are Divine.

Greater gains ahead

*"The Spirit is neither born nor does it
die at any time.
It does not come into being or cease to
exist.
It is unborn, eternal, permanent, and
primeval.
The Spirit is not destroyed when the
body is destroyed."*
– Bhagavad Gita 2.20.

When did you become the child
and I the parent?
When did your body
begin to crumple:
small chinks of decay
blotting the chainmail
that was once your mainstay?

The Play of Life

Now, like a fragile bird
beaten by larger foes,
wings clipped a little
in need of rest and repair.
Your heart still beats
but is weaker now.
The fire in your eyes
-once so fierce as to
singe with one glance-
is softer somehow.

You have retreated a little
it seems to my eye;
forsaken the outer world
for a greater peace within.
Yet there is strength
in this bent frame,
little need for it now
as you sense greater gains ahead.

Rose Petals Floating Downstream

From the child that was
and the parent I have become
I lend my support
on your journey within.
I will hold you when you falter
—yet gently, not grasping.
I will rejoice when you enter
the world again
eyes twinkling with delight,
yet, ever so briefly
before, broken wings repaired,
you venture unto
greater gains ahead.

All the world's a stage

> *"All the world's a stage,*
> *And all the men and women merely*
> *players."*
>
> *- William Shakespeare.*

Splinter-proof days
of tomorrows and yesterdays
cascade into scenes
in God's cosmic play.
Like poems of yesteryear
we delve in and savour
the richness of emotions;
the flavoursome commotions
of Divine streams of light.

Hot and cold
good and evil
shifting sands
of sidewinders' delight.
Life's mediocrity

dulled the senses
like horses drunk on hay:
too lazy to care
that life's great mysteries
were passing us by.

Sweet serenity
may guide us now:
being in the world
but not of it;
actors on stage
yet aware of our place
in Divine motion-picture reality.

And so we play our part
"Till the last scene of all"
holding hands with Infinity
and return of the Soul.

The Missing

> *"Blessed are the hearts that can bend;*
> *they shall never be broken."*
> *-Albert Camus*

Such a windy day today
Divine Mother wants my attention
exhaling her might
in thunderous gusts
down the chimney breast.

But I heed her not.
I'm missing you.
I feel your presence still:
whispering in the walls;
permeating every room.
I see a door ajar
and come in to talk awhile
but all that remains
is the faint refrain
of distant memories,

blown away by daily trials.

The missing you is hard;
it sears through my flesh
to the bone almost.
Each cut a reminder
that you're gone;
each howl of the wind
echoing the pain
of the loss.

Still, I know that this will pass:
for today's storm
is tomorrow's gentle breeze
and this day's trials
tomorrow's memories.
These wounds, too, shall heal
with the grace of Divine Mother.

Mellow in the updraft

No anticipation

of the next

just being in the moment,

a glorious surrender

to what may be.

Effortless stillness,

a pausing in mid-air

like a seabird

caught in an updraft

with little care.

Rose Petals Floating Downstream

Boundless space
where jagged nerves
become mere thoughts
in life's heady race.

I am mellow in the updraft
of my mind
counting each step
as I unwind
into grace.

Like a seabird I soar
carving a path in the silence,
whiter than snowfall,
to illumine the soul.

The Poet

To write is to feel the world
in its essence
every fibre of meaning extracted
to dance across the page,
enveloping the reader
in a languid embrace.
To write is to find oneself
at the core of each word
jostled in turn
by swathes of meaning,
tumbling thought-streams,
sweet rhetoric of wonder.
To write is to walk naked
in the imagination
while closeted unseen,
revealing all for those
who perceive
in lines of poetry
sprouting seedlings of wisdom
disgorged to take flight.

Transformation:

In from the Cold

"And the son said unto him,
Father, I have sinned against heaven,
and in thy sight,
and am no more worthy
to be called thy son." Luke 15:21.

Many years have I spent
adrift in the cold
tormented by storms
whipping at my bones;
railing against
I knew not what
to fill the lack within
to end this ceaseless trek
to give my life new direction.

"And now you're in from the cold…"

I've been looking for You everywhere
in light and dark places

and all the spaces in between.
Material wealth's
languid shadow,
long my beloved bed-fellow,
has been cleansed
by soul's sweet filter.
And concern for the self
above all else
-that velvety cocoon
of over-rated pleasure -
has been consumed
and renewed by the fire.

> *"And now, here you stand,*
>   *my pleading one*
> *grounded in the humility*
>   *of a life undone.*
> *The Angels have heralded*
>   *this joyous day.*
> *But tell me,*
>   *how do I know you will stay?"*

Transformation

Take me in, Father.
I am Your child
My life is in Your hands.
Engulf my soul
in Your heavenly fire.
Breathe life
into the barrenness
of my being,
deathly-chilled
from the cold.
I am ready Lord
for my life to unfold
in Your name,
with Your grace,
by Your desire.

> *"Then cross the hearth dear one*
> *and welcome me into your heart*
> *for I know now we will never part."*

In a Heart-Shaped Lagoon

"Knowing yourself is the beginning
of all wisdom." Aristotle

The pull of the moon
lures me into
the heart-shaped lagoon:
magical gateway
to the realm within.
Stars of many colours
gravitate around me
and crystal-tinged moonbeams
ignite and surround me
in this baptism of light.
Releasing her symphony of
earthly rays;
her ethereal beauty
leads me astray.
Yet I find myself
in this lost lagoon

48

as stroke after stroke
I swim in tune
with the waters.
Twirling with delight
I ascend a cascade
of lyrical light.
Merging with peace
witnessing such joy
bathing in Her
eternal seas of grace.

Dancing Shadows

Dancing shadows
in my room at night.
Whispered kisses
as I turn out the light.
Golden-hued rainbows
streak lazily out of sight.
Dancing with the shadows
burning bright.

Lost treasures of the sacred Divine

"Your vision will become clear
Only when you look into your heart.
Who looks outside, dreams.
Who looks inside, awakens."
-Carl Jung.

Time's eternal stopwatch
is stuck in rewind
to discover lost treasures
of the sacred Divine.
Ancient ways of being
rush headlong into now
to impart forgotten wisdom
to open hearts and minds.

The measure of success?
Our willingness to regress,
then return,

clasping nuggets of truth
tightly to our breast.

Sacred connection
between Mother & Earth
embraces the Goddess within
as we act to heal our world:
hands clasped
in soulful sisterhood;
hearts linked
swollen with love.

Each prayer is a chink of light
in the beloved return to grace.
Each meditation
is a joyful reunion
of the human race.
Each moment of peace
is a memory in time
unlocking the treasures
of the sacred Divine.

Through the Star

Grant me passage

through the star, Lord

to the realm where peace abides.

Help me steer a steady course

to be ever at Thy side.

Meld my soul with Thine:

a tiny ripple in the Infinite Ocean!

Help me span the divide

'tween earth-bound misery

and bliss sublime.

Grant me passage

through the star, Lord.

Drench me in the pool

of Thy heavenly rays.

Feel how my heart aches for Thee!

Immortal soul wings

vibrating towards home.

Hear how my senses sing to Thee!

Transformation

Tender ballads of unforgotten love.

Sweet journey towards grace.

Sweet star of the East.

Steadfast Reminders

"If we don't change, we don't grow.

If we don't grow, we aren't really living."

-Anatole France

My gaze met the beech tree

stalwart of the land

limbs bared by winter's

damp, frosty hand.

I marvelled as each branch

swayed in the breeze

like delicate alveoli

suffused with peace.

My heartbeat aligned

to their slow, steady pace

transfixed in the knowing

that our forms echoed theirs.

Could *I* flex and bend

as winds of change

Transformation

blew through me?

Could *I* remain steady

while all around were at sea?

Could *I* give my breath

so that others might thrive?

Be a steadfast reminder

Of how to be alive?

The House of Brahman #1

I call upon Brahman
to open the door
releasing the serpent
to slumber no more.

I beseech thee, Lord Creator,
to illumine the way
like snowdrops in spring
after winter's decay.

Receive these my roots
in red-ochre-brown
a down-payment
should you wish
for a promise of bliss.

Unfold the envelope
and discard earth-bound woes

that unhindered shall I be
on my onward journey.

Wrap your cloak of strength
around my fragile core.
O Brahman, Lord Creator,
open the door
and release the serpent
to slumber no more.

Joy

The breathless dawn
of an ever-new morn
the effortless grace
of an eagle in flight
cold bones warmed in the sun
purpose freedom love.
A sun-kissed hare
punching the air
a pure white feather
found on the path
the inner silence
the universal Aum
friendship laughter peace.
These are the things
which bring joy
everlasting
hastening my soul
to take flight.

Yesterday's news

I've fashioned a boat out of paper
set it down at the water's side.
Of all my fears and doubts
I've made a little ball
and placed it carefully inside.

A gentle push is all it needs
to send it on its way,
life's troubles soon washed away
like tiny ripples on a pond.

The headlines of yesterday's news
fade with the passage of time
and fears only become real
when given hope to float.
So, start building a boat!

Spell-bound

> *"Supreme bliss comes to a Self-*
> *realized yogi*
> *whose mind is tranquil,*
> *whose desires are under control,*
> *and who is free from sin."*
>
> *-The Bhagavad Gita, 6:27*

Like dew-tossed sunbeams

you pierce my heart

now tears of joy I cry

each droplet an eternal sigh

of love; this beguiling

dance of life,

heaven-sent

and human-spent,

bewitches my being.

For spell-bound am I

by its beauty

by the toing and froing
the living and dying
the truth behind every lie.
This Divine temple
has truth as its seed
a golden tabernacle
unlocked and freed.
So, I let the tears fall:
a Divine gift from within.

Mesmerised am I
by rays of pure bliss
as I edge ever closer
and make my way in.

Freeze-frame

Caught in a freeze-frame
of time-scape expanded:
a shutter-proof moment
of seconds gone awry.
The world and its contents
spun in confusion—
reality viewed through
a different eye.
A zooming-out if you like
an amplification of space
and time.

I sat quite still
watching life spin around.
Full speed ahead it went.
but where was I:
in the past or the present?
"A shifting of boundaries
to encompass something greater."

Transformation

I heard myself say.
Then I rose in slow motion
to begin my day.

The House of Brahman #2

Sweet equanimity of being!
I sail through waters
of fears unrealised
as dreams unrecognised
meander ocean-ward
untroubled by storms.

Copper-toned leaves
dew-drunk and heavy
surrender their bounty
to nature's call;
playing their part in this
dreamlike symphony
of life's eternal cycle
of sacred simplicity.

Trees murmur their secrets
heads touching

Transformation

like gossiping friends
huddled around a fire.
Then, at once,
the mist of my emotions
clears, revealing droplets
of prana suspended mid-air:
like the space before thought.

I see the way ahead now
and the weather is set fair.

An Oasis of light

"It is better to light a candle
than curse the darkness."
-Adlai Stevenson.

Warm Saharan wind
bound for northern climes
sweet breath of life
gives flight to thoughts Divine.

Each cascading whisper
every pore does caress:
an oasis of light
in the desert of the mind.

My tumbleweed thoughts
threaten to unwind
jostled as they are
by Divine Mother's might.

Transformation

Her fiery breath
shimmering without
gently yet firmly
sears the path within.

My whole being imbued
inhales with delight
this life-giving synergy
of love and light.

Drenched, like arid ground
after a rainstorm,
the scars melt away.
I am renewed, repaired:
an Oasis of light.

Jewels

Each letter
a myriad of pixels
poised to become word
and flit across the page.

Each pause
a golden moment
a diadem of meaning
so exquisitely ornate.

Each word
a trail of
breathless pearls
that swoon
in the moonlight
drawn by Her grace.

Each line
soul-gifted

precious jewels
studded on a bed
of ermine.

Each verse
a Universe
of form;
a delicate web
of thought-sprinkles
twinkling into life,
shimmering like diamonds
in a moonless night.

If Thine Eye be Single

> *"The light of the body is the eye:*
> *if therefore thine eye be single,*
> *thy whole body shall be full of light."*
> *Matthew 6:22*

Eyes twinkling
like headlamps dipping
o'er the brow of a hill;
silent messengers
through the mists of time.

Windows on the world
but also to the soul
if we look deeper.

Codeless truths blink
to those who seek
meaning en route.

Transformation

An eternal *clignoter*
Clic, clic, clic.

If thine eye be single
a million stars
Will diffuse into one
and every twist and turn
a delight will be
on this path to eternity.

Prayer / Supplication:

Where dreams take flight

Lift the shroud of fear
from around my eyes
and cast it aside
as a fisherman his net.
Shower me instead
with moonbeams of light
to illumine my heart
my words, my mind.
Merciful Angels
protect me this night
on my sacred journey
where dreams take flight.
Grant that peaceful slumber
may visit me this night
to linger safely in my dreams
till morn's glinting light.

Go swiftly now

I said goodbye to you today
the child that never was
the ties that bound us
so sweetly entwined
through my veins and thoughts.

Such joyful sadness
to send you on your way
that you might bring love
to another one day.

Go swiftly now
lest I turn and reach for you
my child that never was.
May the Angels pave the way
for our souls to meet again
and embrace once more
in eternal love.

Prayer / Supplication

The old woman in me
blesses and thanks you
and sends you on your way
and the young girl in me
can now heal and mend.

In the Garden

*"Father, if thou be willing, remove
this cup from me: nevertheless not
my will, but thine, be done."*

– Luke 22:42.

What place is this

where blossoms cry in pain

dripping sorrowful nectar,

an indelible stain

on my bleeding heart?

O, sweet agony

of tear-soaked solitude

take these my fears

and cast them adrift

on the river of Your compassion.

Hear my lamentations:

the little self begs release.

See, the olive trees sigh

tranquil whispers

and gather me up

in their loving embrace.

These hands have done Thy work;

these feet have trodden

the path laid out for me.

I give myself freely

Thy will *will* be done.

For like the olive

I cannot be without

the sturdy tree;

and like the nectar

I cannot flow without

the blossom at its source.

Pour Thy blessings over me

and hold me in Thy grace,

adored and protected

as dusk's sorrowful rays

extend around my aching core,

calling me to Thee

in ever-increasing waves.

See, my cup overspills
with love for Thee
and rejoices in sweet
blissful union.

Moonbeams sheathed in stardust

(A poem of devotion to one's Guru.)

Take this my love
O Beloved,
wrap it in a bow
of your Divine wisdom
then place it
at the feet of Our Lord.

Take this my smile,
broaden it with
the knowing of your Being
and offer it to God Most High.

Take these my gifts
like moonbeams
sheathed in stardust.
There is no greater bliss
to behold
as restless days unfold

into timeless space
when we shall meet again.

Take this reflection of my soul
and make it your own
sprinkle it across
the night sky
as it journeys home.

Take this my love
O beloved
and place it at
the feet of Our Lord.

Volare!

> *"You need not go to heaven to see God;*
> *nor need you speak loud, as if God were*
> *far away;*
> *nor need you cry for wings like a dove to*
> *fly to Him;*
> *Only be in silence, and you will come*
> *upon God within yourself."*
> *-Saint Teresa of Avila.*

A light breeze singes
the warm air as it passes through
igniting a whispered longing
in my heart.
O that I were a bird
able to touch the ceiling
of the world!
How gladly would I sing
Your praises
if I could be but closer to You.

Rose Petals Floating Downstream

The maturing sun lifts my spirits
and beckons me skyward
yet this earth-bound form
has clipped my wings.
In my dreams I can fly,
create worlds, do anything
I wish: such bliss!

If this breeze could form
into wind
wild, like in a storm,
and lift me airborne
my soul the sweetest song
would sing!

Eternal Sunrise

Many a leaf will fall
blown by the winds of time
before the sun sets
on my love for Thee.

Many a birdcall
will span the divide
before hope is extinguished
by the fire of mankind.

Many a tree will sigh,
many a river will swell.
Yet life will still thrive
in the eternal sunrise
of Thy love.

The Wishing Well

If I could
wave a magic wand
pause time before it's gone.
I'd do it.

If I could
change the will of men
undo the past again.
I'd try it.

If I could
cast a spell so fine
as to soften hearts and minds.
I'd will it.
I'd bottle up that spell
make the whole world
a wishing well:
a shoreless pool of dreams
in a boundless sea of love.

Cast adrift!

> *"Out of the belly of hell cried I,*
> *and thou heardest my voice."*
> *-Book of Jonah 2:2*

Like Jonah in the belly
of the whale am I
cast adrift on an ocean
of uncertainty, as
shuddering waves
of distraction
fracture and crash
from on high,
drowning my focus
with emotion's evil eye.

My oscillating mind,
bewildered and tossed
by waves of thoughts
so reluctant to unwind,
careers port and starboard

like a restless ship's compass
as each wave collides,
buoyed by the stormy sea
of these uneasy times.

Would that I could flee
from this rattling cage of bones,
this self-imposed jail
of emotions unhoned,
before hoisting the sail
and aiming for home!

Lord, I implore Thee
rest by my side;
in peaceful communion
we'll be, Thee and I.

For my shipwrecked soul
yearns for salvation,
emancipation, realization.
And from the belly of the beast

resurrection <u>will</u> be mine!

Help steady my course
keep my aim always in sight.
for am I not a child of God
seeking my Divine birthright?

Save me from this restless plight.
I surrender to Thy will,
with each conscious breath
ever peaceful and still;
I seek only peace
enshrouded in Thy light.

I dip my soul
in the ocean of calm
washed clean by love's might
floating on an endless night,
my whole being is
suffused with Thy light!

Lord, You do not come to me!

"But those who adore Me,
wanting only Me above all else,
and thinking of Me at all times,
I maintain what they already have
and provide what they lack."
-Bhagavad Gita 9:22

Lord, You do not come to me
though I sit and wait each night
in the velvet-clad darkness
of a star-less sky,
sounding Your name
awaiting Your reply.

My beloved Child:
How many times have you thought
of Me this day?
How many prayers have you offered
on bended knee?

How many times have you climbed
the path sublime
to be with Me?

It is I who hast patiently awaited you
but you did not spare the time.
It is I who hast longed for you
to return to My side,
but in the dry riverbed of your mind
your thoughts were little inclined
to reach for Me.

So think of Me often:
each moment, day and night.
And when challenges arise
seek me first, always!
There is no other
who loves you as I do.

Heavenly Father,
like Kabir at his loom

Rose Petals Floating Downstream

I will weave Your name
in all that I do.
Like King Janaka
in his palace ablaze
I will let faith guide me through.
For a chef cannot cook
simply by reading one book
and a lawyer cannot qualify
simply by showing up by and by!
So it is that I
will sound Your name
faithfully, day and night,
and the song of my soul
will echo through time.

Lord, hear my cries—yet faintly.
You *will* come to me, so sweetly,
soft like a whispering breeze
caressing my heart.
You *will* come to me
by and by!

Breathe only hope

I breathe

only hope

that man's strength

be cloaked

in tenderness;

that lives be

not crushed

but lifted;

that making love

be sharing peace.

And I breathe

only hope

that smog

dissipates;

that strangers

relate

to one another

like kin.

Still I breathe

only hope

that egos

be toppled

from pedestals

of hate and pride;

that *all* shall be free

to thrive.

Till my last breath

I believe

only hope

shall I breathe.

About the Author:

Anita Neilson is an author, spiritual poet and blogger. A graduate in 3 modern languages, she travelled, lived and worked in Europe before careers in business and education in Scotland. She is now a self-employed writer, contributing to many mind body spirit and chronic illness publications.

Anita lives in the lush, verdant countryside of Ayrshire, in the west of Scotland, where the beauty and diversity of the natural world provide inspiration for much of her writing. Kindness, compassion and leading a positive, spiritual life are upmost to her. Anita has Fibromyalgia and M.E. (Chronic Fatigue Syndrome) and her husband is her care giver and inspiration for many an act of kindness.

Other books by the Author: *Acts of Kindness from your Armchair* (Ayni Books); *Soul Murmurs* (O-Books).

Contributing Author to *Goddess: When She Rules* (Golden Dragonfly Press).

Her blog and poetry aim to teach others:

- how illness can be a blessing, presenting us as it does with opportunities for soul growth (such as increased compassion for others' suffering);
- how we can distract the mind from pain and fatigue through the healing power of positive thoughts and words; and
- how we can all make a meaningful contribution to the world simply by reconnecting with our inner compassion and love.

Connect with Anita:

http://anitaneilson.com
http://www.facebook.com/AnitaNeilsonAuthor
http://www.instagram.com/soulmurmurs

Other books by the Author:

Acts of Kindness from your Armchair, Ayni Books 2017. ISBN: 978-1-78535-617-9

An exploration of how we can make a meaningful contribution to the world through simple acts of kindness, all easily done from home. The book acts as a practical guide to the ways in which thoughts, words and acts of kindness, both inward and towards the wider world, can create real change. It leads us on a journey from compassionate self-analysis and meditation; kindness towards others both in person and online; kindness towards the animal kingdom and finally caring for the planet—one little step after another! This toolkit of ideas and practices arose from the author's personal experiences in her quest to find a new purpose in life, despite health limitations, through the power of kindness.

"We can all make a difference, regardless of any 'limitations' we may have, whatever our circumstances. In my experience all 'big' things happen through lots of small things, and this book is a great reminder of the big difference that small everyday acts of kindness can make." Karen Darke MBE, Athlete and Adventurer, Paralympic Champion 2016. Author of *If You Fall* and *Boundless*.

"A spiritual guidebook for harmonious living." Catherine L. Schweig, Editor of *Bhakti Blossoms, Journey of the Heart* and others.

"Inspires the reader to achieve a happier, more fulfilled living and open up to positivity, peace and natural wellbeing." Fotoula Adrimi, Director ISIS School of Holistic Health.

"This is also great for other people who want to help but have no idea where to start." Dawn's Reviews.

Goddess When She Rules, Golden Dragonfly Press 2017. ISBN: 9780998976655

Contributing Author in this extraordinary collection of poetry and prose penned by spiritual women across the globe in an exploration of what the Goddess energy signifies to them.

COMING SOON! (July 2019)

Soul Murmurs: Seasonal words of spiritual wisdom to enlighten the soul, O-Books. ISBN: 978-1-78904-111-8

A must-have collection of poetry and prose imbued with spiritual wisdom from east and west. Gathered under seasonal headings to echo the eternal cycle of life, each page resonates with peace and calm, offering comfort and moments of reflection in a fast-moving world.

Advance praise for Soul Murmurs:

"Anita Neilson's compassionates heart is evident as it leaps from the page, as she beckons us all: the ill, the wounded, the lost, and the seeker of Divinity, to take her hand and walk with her on a journey through the seasons. Seasons of the earth, seasons of the heart and emotions, all the circles and cycles of life. This elegant collection of seasonal prose and poetry is a balm for the soul."

Janavi Held, Poet and Author of *Letters to my oldest friend.*

"*Soul Murmurs* leads the reader on a beautifully sublime spiritual metamorphosis in tune with the ebb and rhythm of the seasons. The author's words transfer a calm wisdom that speaks of an inner resilience born of her own transformation."

Jenny Light, inspirational speaker, healer and author, *Divine Meditations-26 Spiritual Qualities of the Bhagavad Gita.*

"Anita Neilson's words radiate joy and appreciation for the great dance of impermanence. From cleaning the closets of our mind in Spring, to receiving Winter's invitation as darkness falls to get quiet and still, *Soul Murmurs* offers practical tips, insights, and gorgeous spiritual poems that we can dip into all year long."

Mariah McKenzie, Author of *More, Journey to Mystical Union through the sacred and the profane*.

Note to Reader:

Thank you for purchasing *Rose Petals Floating Downstream*. I hope that your soul feels enlightened and that you have gained as much from its reading as I did from its creation. If you have a few moments, please feel free to add your review of the book on your favourite online site for feedback. Much love.

Anita Neilson

31417291R00065

Printed in Poland
by Amazon Fulfillment
Poland Sp. z o.o., Wrocław